D1372503

Fish

The Taunton Press

ACADEMIA BARILLA
AMBASSADOR OF ITALIAN GASTRONOMY
THROUGHOUT THE WORLD

Academia Barilla is a global movement toward the protection, development and promotion of authentic regional Italian culture and cuisine.
With the concept of Food as Culture at our core, Academia Barilla offers a 360° view of Italy. Our comprehensive approach includes:

- a state-of-the-art culinary center in Parma, Italy;
- gourmet travel programs and hands-on cooking classes;
- the world's largest Italian gastronomic library and historic menu collection;
- a portfolio of premium artisan food products;
- global culinary certification programs;
- custom corporate services and training;
- team building activities;
- and a vast assortment of Italian cookbooks.

Thank you and we look forward to welcoming you in Italy soon!

CONTENTS

EDITED BY
ACADEMIA BARILLA

PHOTOGRAPHS
ALBERTO ROSSI

RECIPES BY
CHEF MARIO GRAZIA
CHEF LUCA ZANGA

TEXT BY
MARIAGRAZIA VILLA

ACADEMIA BARILLA EDITORIAL COORDINATION
CHATO MORANDI
ILARIA ROSSI
REBECCA PICKRELL

GRAPHIC DESIGN
PAOLA PIACCO

JUST AS YOU NEED TO KNOW MUSIC
WELL IN ORDER TO PLAY CHOPIN,
TO COOK A FISH YOU NEED TO KNOW
THE QUALITY OF ITS FLESH.

GUALTIERO MARCHESI

FISH

The richness of the sea surrounding the Italian peninsula, as well as the rivers and lakes punctuating its inland territories, have ensured that fish has always played an important role in the Italian culinary tradition. Over the centuries, the people living by the sea or near freshwater basins learned to cook fish, as well as to conserve it by salting or drying. Today, the collection of recipes is priceless, and the variety of fish that can be brought to the table truly vast. For as many species as there are, both freshwater and saltwater, there are recipes to bring out their best qualities. There are fish of white flesh, pink flesh or red flesh, lending themselves to a multitude of preparations—often simply a few herbs, to best appreciate the seafood's fragrance and flavor. There are crustaceans, with especially delicate flesh, and the very humble—and very flavorful—shellfish, such as mussels, clams and scallops.

Fish is truly one of the stars of Italian cuisine. It can be enjoyed steamed, with a bit of lemon juice and a drizzle of extra-virgin olive oil, or in a simple seafood salad, or it can be used in more extravagant recipes, such as delicious fish soups. It is also used in appetizers and starter courses, and more and more it is substituting for meat in main course dishes, at restaurants and at home. These factors make it one of the cornerstones of the so-called Mediterranean diet, increasingly recommended by nutritionists for its balance and documented health benefits. It was even included on UNESCO's 2010 Representative List of the Cultural Heritage of Humanity.

Academia Barilla, an international center dedicated

to the preservation and promotion of Italian cuisine, has selected 40 extraordinary recipes of fish-based main course dishes from the traditions of the *Bel Paese* (the "beautiful country," as Italians call their home). They are dishes with a great deal of lightness, but with a truly special flavor. Think, for example, of the sublime Sea Bass in Acqua Pazza, or the tasty Mussels Marinara. There is the satisfying cuttlefish with peas, and the delicate octopus with potatoes; the inviting seafood skewers with Salmoriglio sauce, or the scented sea bream with a mantle of porcini mushrooms.

Some of the recipes have been carefully selected from the vast heritage of regional cuisines, such as the famous Vicenza-style cod, a veritable delicacy for gourmets; the Adriatic Fisherman's Broth, practically a twin of the fish soup eaten on the Tyrrhenian Sea; and the intriguing Livorno-style dogfish, with its distinctive tomato sauce.

Other recipes, however, are delightfully Italian for their use of excellent typical local products—from Pantelleria capers to the balsamic vinegar of Modena, from the Sicilian Bronte pistachios to wild mushrooms—and for the culinary art of the *Bel Paese* that knows how to create true masterpieces of flavor: a salad of swordfish in wild fennel; the slice of amberjack crusted with almonds and pistachios, served with an artichoke salad; the seared filet of tuna with eggplant and zucchini caponata. This is a dip into the delicacies of the Mediterranean that Italian cuisine has always celebrated with inspiration and grace.

FRIED ANCHOVIES

Preparation time: 30 minutes   Cooking time: 5 minutes   Difficulty: easy

4 SERVINGS

14 oz. (400 g) **fresh anchovies**
1/3 cup (50 g) **Italian "00" flour** or all-purpose flour
3 large **eggs**
2 1/4 cups (300 g) **breadcrumbs**
Extra-virgin olive oil, for frying
Salt to taste

Clean the anchovies, removing the heads, innards and bones. Slice them in half lengthwise, butterfly them, then rinse and dry them. Dredge the anchovies in the flour, then dip them in the beaten egg and coat them with breadcrumbs.
Heat the oil in a large skillet over medium-high heat until shimmering. Fry the anchovies until golden brown and then remove them with a perforated spoon.
Place them on paper towels to dry and sprinkle them with salt.
Serve them in cones or pouches of paper or foil.

CITRUS-MARINATED ANCHOVIES
WITH FENNEL SALAD

Preparation time: 30 minutes plus 1 day to marinate   Difficulty: easy

4 SERVINGS

1 lb. 5 oz. (600 g) **fresh anchovies**
1 **lemon**
1 **orange**
3 tbsp. plus 2 tsp. (50 ml) **extra-virgin olive oil**
1 **sprig fresh thyme**
1/4 cup **roughly chopped fennel fronds**
Salt and pepper to taste
1 1/2 lbs. (700 g) **fennel**, or about 3 bulbs

Clean the anchovies, removing the bones and innards. Zest the lemon and
orange with a vegetable peeler, and mince the zest. Juice the lemon
and orange and set aside.
Strip the thyme leaves from the stem. Arrange half the thyme and chopped
fennel fronds in a bowl. Add the minced citrus zest and a drizzle
of extra-virgin olive oil.
Place the anchovies on top of the herb-citrus mixture. Cover them with the
remaining herbs, the lemon and orange juices and a pinch of salt and pepper.
Cover the bowl of anchovies with plastic wrap and marinate for a
full day in the refrigerator.
Clean the fennel bulb and slice it thinly. Rinse it well in cold water and drain.
Arrange the anchovies on a plate and serve with the fennel.

SALT COD VICENZA-STYLE

Preparation time: 20 minutes   Cooking time: 4 1/2 hours   Difficulty: medium

4 SERVINGS

1 lb. (500 g) **dried salt cod** *(baccalà)*
2 cups plus 2 tbsp. (500 ml) **extra-virgin olive oil**
8 3/4 oz. (250 g) **onion***, or 1 large, finely chopped*
3 **anchovy fillets***, rinsed well and drained*
Salt and pepper *to taste*
All-purpose flour*, as needed*
2 oz. (50 g) **fresh parsley***, chopped*
2 cups plus 2 tbsp. (500 ml) **milk**
1 oz. (28 g) **Parmigiano-Reggiano cheese***, grated (about 3-4 tbsp)*
1 1/2 cups (250 g) **cornmeal**
Unsalted butter*, as needed*

One day ahead, rinse the salt cod, put it in a large bowl and cover with cold water. Cover with plastic wrap and refrigerate overnight, changing the water several times.

Heat 2 tablespoons of oil in a large skillet and sauté the onion until tender. Add the anchovies and cook until fragrant.

Cut the salt cod into pieces, season with salt and pepper. Dredge the cod in the flour and place in a saucepan. Cover with the sautéed onion, the parsley, the grated Parmigiano-Reggiano, the milk and the rest of the oil. Cook over a low flame for about 4 hours.

Serve with soft polenta. To make it, gradually whisk the cornmeal in a steady stream into about 5 cups of salted boiling water together with about 1 teaspoon of butter (preferably using a copper pan). Cook the polenta for about 30 minutes, stirring frequently.

SALT COD WITH POTATOES
AND SAFFRON

Preparation time: 40 minutes   Cooking time: 10 minutes   Difficulty: easy

4 SERVINGS

1 1/2 lbs. (680 g) **dried salt cod** *(baccalà)*
10 1/2 oz. (300 g) **potatoes**, *peeled*
Pinch of **saffron**
1 tbsp. (4 g) **chopped parsley**, *plus more for garnish*
1 **fresh bay leaf**
5 tbsp. (70 g) **unsalted butter**
Cayenne pepper *to taste, plus more for garnish*
Salt *to taste*
Lemon slices, *for garnish*

One day ahead, rinse the salt cod, put it in a large bowl and cover with cold water. Cover with plastic wrap and refrigerate overnight, changing the water several times.

Boil the potatoes (whole) with the saffron and bay leaf in a pot of slightly salted boiling water (a little over 1 quart); cook the potatoes so that they maintain a bit of their consistency, and keep them warm in the cooking water.

Meanwhile, cut the cod into slices, season with salt, and sauté in a skillet with the butter. Season with cayenne pepper as desired.

Cook for about 10 minutes, turning over halfway through cooking. Toward the end, sprinkle with chopped parsley.

Drain the potatoes, cut them into rather thick rounds, and distribute them on the individual plates. Arrange the slices of cod over the potatoes; garnish with cayenne pepper, parsley, and lemon slices.

SEA BASS IN "ACQUA PAZZA"

Preparation time: 15 minutes   Cooking time: 20 minutes   Difficulty: easy

4 SERVINGS

3 lbs. 5 oz. (1 1/2 kg) **sea bass fillets**
5 oz. (150 g) **onion,** *or about 2 small, thinly sliced*
8 oz. (250 g) **cherry tomatoes,** *or about 15*
3 1/2 tbsp. (50 ml) **extra-virgin olive oil**
5 **fresh basil leaves**
2 cloves **garlic**
3/4 cup plus 1 1/2 tbsp. (200 ml) **water**
Salt and pepper *to taste*

In a large straight-sided skillet, sauté the onion, garlic and basil in the olive oil. Add the tomatoes and water and simmer for 10 minutes. Season the fish with salt and pepper, then place it in the *acqua pazza* ("crazy water") and cook until flaky and cooked through.

BAKED SEA BASS

Preparation time: 20 minutes   Cooking time: 12-15 minutes   Difficulty: medium

4 SERVINGS

2 **whole sea bass**, filleted (500-600 g or 1 1/3 lbs. each)
6 oz. (200 g) **potatoes**, peeled and cut into wedges
2 oz. (80 g) **salt-packed capers**, rinsed well and drained
20 **small black olives**, preferably Taggiasca
1/3 cup plus 1 1/2 tbsp. (100 ml) **extra-virgin olive oil**
1 tbsp. (4 g) **chopped fresh parsley**
4 **sprigs fresh rosemary**
4 **fresh sage leaves**
Salt and pepper to taste

Cook the potatoes in a large pot of boiling salted water for 5 minutes, then drain.
Place four parchment squares on work surface. Divide the fish fillets among the
parchment squares and season with salt and pepper. Distribute the olives,
capers, and potato wedges over the sea bass. Top each fillet with the rosemary
and sage. Drizzle with the oil and fold parchment over fish, folding and crimping
edges tightly to seal and enclose filling completely. Wrap the paper packets
individually in aluminum foil and bake at 350°F (180°C) for 12 to 15 minutes.
Serve the sea bass fillets with a sprinkling of freshly chopped parsley.

GROUPER MATALOTTA-STYLE

Preparation time: 25 minutes   Cooking time: 15 minutes   Difficulty: easy

4 SERVINGS

1/2 cup (60 g) **all-purpose flour**
1 3/4 lb. (800 g) **grouper fillets**
3 1/2 tbsp. (50 ml) **extra-virgin olive oil**
3 1/2 oz. (100 g) **onion**, *or about 1 1/2 small, thinly sliced*
1 clove **garlic**, *thinly sliced*
1/2 cup (100 ml) **white wine**
7 oz. (200 g) **tomatoes**, *quartered*
1/2 cup (100 ml) **fish broth**
1 **fresh bay leaf**

3 1/2 oz. (100 g) **button mushrooms**, *thinly sliced*
Salt and pepper *to taste*
1/3 oz. (8 g) **fresh parsley**, *chopped*

FOR THE TOPPING
3 1/2 oz. (100 g) **zucchini**, *about 1/2 medium, sliced*
2 3/4 oz. (80 g) **bell peppers**, *or 1 small, cut into small dice*
1/4 cup (30 g) **slivered almonds**

Place the flour in a baking pan with low edges. Lightly flour the grouper fillets.
Heat the oil in a large skillet and sauté the garlic and half of the onion for 1 minute.
Add the fish and fry gently. Add the white wine and simmer until it evaporates.
Add the tomatoes, fish broth, bay leaf and mushrooms, and season with salt and pepper. Add the parsley and cook over low heat for 5 minutes.
In a medium skillet over high heat sauté the remaining onion, zucchini and a pinch of salt. Add the peppers and cook until tender. Season to taste. Stir in the almonds.
Arrange the fillets on a serving dish, then top with the vegetables.

HAKE CROQUETTES

Preparation time: 40 minutes   Cooking time: 5 minutes   Difficulty: medium

4 SERVINGS

8 oz. (220 g) **potatoes**, or about 1 medium, peeled and cut into large chunks

1/3 cup plus 1 1/2 tbsp. (100 ml) **extra-virgin olive oil**

3 1/2 oz. (100 g) **onions**, or about 1 1/2 small, finely chopped

14 oz. (400 g) **hake fillets**

Salt and pepper to taste

5 oz. (140 g) **sliced white bread**, or about 6 slices

1/2 cup (30 g) **finely chopped fresh parsley**

3/4 cup (50 g) **finely chopped fresh basil**

1 tbsp. (4 g) **minced fresh chives**

3 large **eggs**, lightly beaten

3 1/2 oz. (100 g) **breadcrumbs**, or about 3/4 cup

Vegetable oil for frying, as needed

Balsamic vinegar to taste

Boil the potatoes in a pot of lightly salted water until tender. Drain the potatoes and mash them. Drizzle 1 1/2 tablespoons olive oil in a pan and sauté the onions over high heat until tender. Add the hake fillets; using a wooden spoon break up the fillets while they cook. When the fish is done, transfer it to a large bowl. Mix in the mashed potatoes, season with salt and pepper and let it cool.

Remove the crust from the sliced bread and break up the bread.

Put it in a food processor with the blade attachment, along with the herbs, and blend until the mixture is uniformly green. Shape the fish mixture into 1-inch-wide (3 cm) cylinders. Divide them into 2-inch (5 cm) lengths. Dip them in the breadcrumbs, then the beaten egg and then the herbed bread. Heat a large skillet with oil until hot and shimmering. Fry the croquettes until golden brown on both sides. Remove them with a slotted spoon and place them on paper towels to drain. Serve on a bed of lettuce and top with a few drops of balsamic vinegar.

26

FILLET OF SEA BASS

Preparation time: 20 minutes   Cooking time: 15 minutes   Difficulty: easy

4 SERVINGS

1 lb. 2 oz. (500 g) **whole sea bass**
1/4 cup (60 ml) **extra-virgin olive oil**
Salt and pepper *to taste*
7 oz. (200 g) **cherry tomatoe**s, *halved*
2 tbsp. (20 g) **salt-packed capers**, *rinsed well*
3 1/2 oz. (100 g) **green olives**, *or about 36*
Chopped fresh parsley *to taste*

Clean the sea bass, remove the skin, cut into fillets and season with salt and pepper. Lightly oil a pan with 1 tablespoon of oil and add the fillets. Top with the tomatoes and capers and season with salt and pepper. Drizzle with the remaining oil, cover the pan with a lid and cook for 15 minutes over low heat or in a 350°F (180°C) oven, adding a little water if necessary. Towards the end of the cooking time, add the olives and sprinkle with the parsley.

SEARED TUNA FILLET

Preparation time: 30 minutes   Cooking time: 15 minutes   Difficulty: easy

4 SERVINGS

14 oz. (400 g) **eggplant**, *or about 3/4 medium*
Salt and pepper *to taste*
2/3 cup (150 ml) **extra-virgin olive oil**
2 oz. (56 g) **onion** *or about 3/4 small, cut into small dice*
2 oz. (56 g) **celery**, *or about 1 1/2 medium stalks, cut into fine dice*
3 1/2 oz. (100 g) **zucchini**, *or about 1 small, cut into small dice*
1 1/2 tbsp. (20 g) **raisins**

2 tbsp. (30 g) **capers**
2 tbsp. (30 g) **pine nuts**
1 oz. (28 g) **black olives**, *or about 6 large*
3 1/2 oz. (100 g) **crushed tomatoes**
1 tsp. (5 ml) **vinegar**
1 tbsp. (10 g) **sugar**
1/2 oz. (15 g) **pistachios** *or about 22*
1 **bunch fresh basil**, *torn into pieces*
1 lb. (450 g) **tuna fillet**
4 **sprigs fresh thyme**
1 clove **garlic**

Rinse and cube the eggplant, then put it in a colander, salt it lightly and allow it to drain for about 30 minutes. Heat 1/2 cup of the olive oil in a large skillet until hot and shimmering and fry the eggplant until browned. Remove eggplant from the skillet with a slotted spoon and place on a plate lined with paper towels to drain. Add the onion to the pan and sauté until tender, then add the zucchini and let them brown lightly. Add the raisins, capers, pine nuts and olives. Add the crushed tomatoes and fried eggplant and season with salt and pepper to taste. Let everything cook for a few minutes. Add the vinegar and sugar, and then finally add the whole pistachios and basil. Cook for a few minutes until the flavors meld together. Cut the tuna into thick slices and season it with salt and pepper. Drizzle the remaining olive oil in a nonstick pan and heat it with the thyme and whole garlic clove. Sear the tuna (1 to 2 minutes on each side) and serve it with the vegetables on the side.

MONKFISH SALAD

Preparation time: 30 minutes   Cooking time: 5 minutes   Difficulty: easy

4 SERVINGS

7 oz. (200 g) **mixed greens**, torn
1 3/4 oz. (50 g) **carrot**, or about 1 small
3 oz. (85 g) **fennel** or about 1/3 bulb
2 lbs. 3 oz. (1 kg) **monkfish fillets**,
    sliced 1/8-1/4 inch (0.5 cm) thick
1/2 oz. (22 g) **pickled capers**, or about
    2 tbsp., rinsed
1 tbsp. (4 g) **fresh minced parsley**
1/3 cup plus 1 1/2 tbsp. (100 ml) **extra-
    virgin olive oil**

1/2 tsp. (3 ml) **balsamic vinegar**,
    preferably aged Modena
Salt and white pepper to taste
4-5 **fresh mint leaves**, torn
12 **fresh chive leaves**, sliced
4-5 **fresh basil leaves**, torn
1 sprig of **marjoram**, leaves picked

In a large skillet heat one-quarter of the oil over medium heat and sauté the
monkfish until golden brown and cooked through. Season generously
with salt and pepper.
Toss the greens with the mint, chives, basil and marjoram and arrange in the
center of the plate. Place the fish on top with the capers and minced parsley.
Season with balsamic vinegar, olive oil, salt and pepper.

MIMOSA SALAD WITH MACKEREL

Preparation time: 50 minutes   Difficulty: easy

4 SERVINGS

4 large **eggs**
14 oz. (400 g) **potatoes**
3 1/2 oz. (100 g) **mixed salad greens**
14 oz. (400 g) **fresh whole mackerel**, *scaled and gutted*
Generous 3/8 cup (100 ml) **extra-virgin olive oil**
Red wine vinegar
Salt and pepper *to taste*

Put the eggs in a pan and cover them with water.
Bring to a boil over high heat and simmer for 8 to 10 minutes. Immediately plunge them in cold water to stop the cooking process and to make them easier to peel. Peel the eggs, then separate the yolks from the whites (which are not used in this recipe). Scrub the potatoes and boil them in their skins in plenty of salted water until tender when pricked with a fork. Drain potatoes and leave to cool, then peel and cut into slices about 1/4 inch (5 mm) thick. Season the insides of the mackerel with salt and pepper, then pour a little oil over them. Set an oven rack 6 inches from the top element and heat the broiler to medium. Broil on both sides until cooked through, remove from the oven, let cool slightly then fillet the mackerel. Season the salad greens with salt, pepper and vinegar, and arrange them on individual plates. Add the sliced potatoes and filleted mackerel. Season with salt and oil. Press the hard-cooked yolks through a sieve and sprinkle over the plate.

SEA BREAM PUGLIA-STYLE

Preparation time: 30 minutes   Cooking time: 15-20 minutes   Difficulty: medium

4 SERVINGS

1 **whole sea bream**, 2 lbs. 3 oz. (1 kg) (or striped bass)
10 1/2 oz. (300 g) **potatoes** or about 2 small, peeled and thinly sliced
1 3/4 oz. (50 g) **Pecorino cheese**, grated or about 1/2 cup
1 clove **garlic**, minced
1 tbsp. (4 g) **chopped fresh parsley**
3 tbsp. (40 ml) **extra-virgin olive oil**
Salt and pepper to taste

Clean, scale and fillet the fish.
Bring a large pot of salted water to a boil over high heat, add the potatoes and
cook for 5 minutes. Drain well. Grease a pan (or line it with parchment paper)
and cover the bottom with a layer of potatoes. Combine the Pecorino, garlic and
parsley and sprinkle half the mixture evenly over the potatoes.
Arrange a layer of sea bream fillets and sprinkle them with salt and pepper.
Cover them with the remaining half of the ingredients, being careful to place
the potato slices gently. Drizzle with olive oil and bake at 400°F (200°C)
for about 15 to 20 minutes.

SEA BREAM
WITH PORCINI MUSHROOMS

Preparation time: 20 minutes   Cooking time: 8 minutes   Difficulty: medium

4 SERVINGS

Four 4 1/2-oz. (130 g) **gilthead sea bream fillets** *(or sea bass)*
3 1/2 tbsp. (50 ml) **extra-virgin olive oil**
10 1/2 oz. (300 g) **porcini mushroom caps**, *sliced 1/16 in. (1-2 mm) thick*
Salt and pepper *to taste*

Arrange the fish in a lightly oiled baking pan. Season with salt and pepper and cover with the mushroom slices, placing them so that they overlap slightly. Drizzle with olive oil and bake at 350°F (180°C) for 7 to 8 minutes.

DOGFISH LIVORNO-STYLE

Preparation time: 30 minutes   Cooking time: 20 minutes   Difficulty: easy

4 SERVINGS

1 3/4 lbs. (800 g) **dogfish steaks** (or halibut steaks)
1 lb. (500 g) **ripe tomatoes**, or about 4 medium
5 oz. (150 g) **onions** or about 2 small, cut into small dice
1/3 cup plus 1 1/2 tbsp (100 ml) **white wine**
1/4 cup (60 ml) **extra-virgin olive oil**
1 clove **garlic**, minced
1 tbsp. (4 g) **minced fresh parsley**
Salt and pepper to taste

Prepare the tomatoes by making an X-shaped incision on the bottom of each
tomato and blanching them in boiling water for 10 to 15 seconds. Immediately
dip the tomatoes in ice water, then peel them, remove the seeds, and dice them.
Heat the oil in a pan and sauté the minced garlic and onion until tender but not at
all browned. Add the fish steaks and let them cook for about 3 to 4 minutes. Pour
in the white wine, let it evaporate and add the tomatoes. Season with salt and
pepper to taste, turn the fish and let it finish cooking, about 3 minutes more.
If necessary, add a bit of water. Add the parsley at the very end, just before
removing from the heat.

SWORDFISH
IN SALMORIGLIO SAUCE

Preparation time: 20 minutes   Cooking time: 5 minutes   Difficulty: easy

4 SERVINGS

1 1/3 lbs. (600 g) **swordfish fillet**, *cut into four slices*
2 **lemons**, *juiced*
1 clove **garlic**, *chopped*
1 tbsp. (4 g) **fresh parsley**, *chopped*
1 tsp. **fresh oregano**, *chopped*
7/8 cup (200 ml) **extra-virgin olive oil**
3 1/2 tbsp. (50 ml) **hot water**
Salt and pepper *to taste*

For the salmoriglio sauce: Put the oil, lemon juice and water in a bowl and whisk together. Add the garlic, parsley and oregano, then emulsify the sauce in a bowl over a pan of gently simmering water, whisking constantly for 5 to 6 minutes. Brush the slices of fish with the salmoriglio sauce and cook on a medium-high griddle or grill for a few minutes, moistening with the sauce as the fish cooks. Season with salt and pepper. Brush with the sauce once again and serve.

MONKFISH IN LEEK SAUCE

Preparation time: 40 minutes   Cooking time: 25 minutes   Difficulty: easy

4 SERVINGS

1 1/2 lbs. (1 1/2 kg) **monkfish fillets**
4 3/4 tbsp. (70 ml) **extra-virgin olive oil**
7 oz. (200 g) **ripe tomatoes**, *halved*
1 lb. (500 g) **leeks** *(white part only)*
2 cloves **garlic**, *sliced*
1 **bunch fresh parsley**, *chopped*
1 lb. (500 g) **pitted black olives**
3 cups (700 ml) **water**
1 tbsp. plus 1 tsp. (20 ml) **white vinegar**
Crushed red pepper *to taste*
Salt and pepper *to taste*

Slice the leeks into round slices, then rinse well under running water. Boil the water and the vinegar and blanch the leeks in it for a few seconds, then drain and dry. Cut the monkfish fillets into uniformly sized pieces, and blanch for a few minutes in a large pot of boiling salted water. Drain and set aside.
Soften the leeks and the garlic in the oil over medium heat, add a pinch of crushed red pepper, the tomatoes and the parsley, and bring to a boil.
Lower the heat, add the monkfish and the olives and cook over low heat for 15 minutes. Before serving, season with salt and a little freshly ground pepper.

SALMON
WITH POTATOES AND EGGS

Preparation time: 30 minutes   Cooking time: 7-8 minutes   Difficulty: easy

4 SERVINGS

1 lb. 3 oz. (600 g) **salmon,** *cut into 4 fillets*
1 lb. (500 g) **potatoes**
2 large **eggs**
1 tbsp. (4 g) **chopped fresh parsley**
3 1/2 tbsp. (50 g) **unsalted butter**
Salt and pepper *to taste*

Put the eggs in a pan and cover them with water. Bring to a boil over high heat and simmer for 8 to 10 minutes. Immediately plunge them in cold water to stop the cooking process and to make them easier to peel. Peel the eggs and then press them through a fine-mesh sieve. Set aside.
Peel the potatoes and make little potato balls using a melon baller or small scoop with a diameter of 1 inch (2 1/2 cm). Cook the potatoes in a large pot of boiling salted water for 5 minutes.
Season the salmon with salt and pepper.
Melt the butter in a large skillet and when it begins to foam, brown the salmon on both sides. Add the potatoes and bake in the oven at 350°F (180°C) for 7 to 8 minutes. After removing from the oven, sprinkle each serving with the eggs and parsley and serve.

JOHN DORY
WITH EGGPLANT PURÉE

Preparation time: 50 minutes   Cooking time: 10 minutes   Difficulty: easy

4 SERVINGS

1 lb. 3 oz. (600 g) **John Dory fillet** *(sole or flounder can be substituted)*
14 oz. (400 g) **tomatoes**, *or about 2 large*
2 1/4 lbs. (1 kg) **eggplant**, *or about 2*
2 1/2 oz. (75 g) **red onion**, *or about 1 small, thinly sliced*
2 cloves **garlic**, *thinly sliced*
1 **bunch fresh basil**
2/3 cup (150 ml) **extra-virgin olive oil**
Salt and pepper *to taste*

Heat the oven to 400°F (200°C).
With a paring knife, pierce eggplant a few times and insert a garlic slice in each slit.
Wrap the eggplant in aluminum foil, and bake for 40 minutes. When cooked,
purée the eggplant with 3 1/2 tablespoons (50 ml) of the olive oil and a pinch of
salt. Peel the tomatoes, remove the seeds, and dice them. Blend the basil leaves
with 3 1/2 tablespoons (50 ml) of olive oil and a pinch of salt.
Season the fish fillets with salt and pepper. Heat the remaining oil in a large
skillet and sauté the fish until golden brown and cooked through. Transfer to a
plate. Sauté the onion and tomatoes until tender. Arrange the fish and eggplant
purée on each plate, and drizzle the basil oil on top.

BECCAFICO SARDINES

Preparation time: 40 minutes   Cooking time: 20 minutes   Difficulty: medium

4 SERVINGS

1 lb. (500 g) **sardines**
3 1/2 oz. (100 g) **dried breadcrumbs**, *or about 3/4 cup*
2 **salt-packed anchovies**, *desalted and finely chopped*
2/3 oz. (20 g) **pine nuts**
2/3 oz. (20 g) **raisins**
1 tbsp. (4 g) **fresh parsley**, *chopped*
3 1/2 tbsp. (50 ml) **extra-virgin olive oil**
Fresh bay leaves *to taste*
Salt and pepper *to taste*

If using fresh sardines, remove the heads and the innards. Remove the bones but leave the tail. Rinse and dry them. If using canned sardines, rinse and dry. Soak the raisins in lukewarm water for about 15 minutes and then drain them well. Heat 2 1/2 tablespoons of the oil in a skillet, add the breadcrumbs and sauté until they start to brown. Let cool and then add the parsley, pine nuts, raisins and anchovies, season with salt and pepper, and mix together well. Cut the sardines lengthwise and butterfly them. Put a little of the mixture on each sardine so that the skin remains on the outside, and then roll them up, starting from the head, so that the tail is left outside. Secure the rolls with a toothpick. Place the sardines on the bay leaves in an oiled baking pan. Drizzle with the remaining oil and bake in the oven at 350°F (180°C) for about 20 minutes.

TUNA TARTARE

Preparation time: 35 minutes   Difficulty: easy

4 SERVINGS

12 oz. (350 g) **very fresh tuna steak**
1 oz. (30 g) **shallots**, *or about 3 tbsp. minced*
1 3/4 oz (50 g) **pickled capers**, *or about 1/4 cup plus 1 tbsp.*
1 lb. (500 g) **eggplant**, *or about 1 medium*
3 1/2 oz. (100 g) **onions** *or about 1 1/2 small, finely chopped*
1/4 cup plus 1 tbsp. (75 ml) **white wine vinegar**
2 1/2 tsp. (10 g) **sugar**
A few **fresh mint** *and* **basil leaves**
1/3 cup plus 1 1/2 tbsp. (100 ml) **extra-virgin olive oil**
Salt and pepper *to taste*

Sauté the onion in a saucepan over low heat with a few tablespoons of oil. Cube the eggplant and sauté it in a nonstick pan with a bit of oil. Season it with salt and pepper and add it to the onion. Add 2/3 cup of vinegar along with the sugar. Let it finish cooking, seasoning with mint and basil. Strain the capers, mince them and mix them with a bit of oil.
Dice the tuna and season it with salt, pepper, minced shallot and the remaining oil. Serve the tuna tartare with the eggplant and the caper sauce, and garnish with basil leaves, if desired.

SWORDFISH STEAK
WITH LEMON AND CAPERS

Preparation time: 20 minutes   Cooking time: 10 minutes   Difficulty: easy

4 SERVINGS

14 oz. (400 g) **swordfish steaks**
1 oz. (25 g) **salt-packed capers**, *or about 3 tbsp.*
5 oz. (150 g) **mâche**
2 **lemons**
3 1/2 tbsp. (50 ml) **extra-virgin olive oil**
Salt and pepper *to taste*

Slice the swordfish into 4 pieces. Season them with salt and pepper on both sides and arrange them in a lightly oiled baking pan.

Remove the peel and pith from the lemons. Working over a bowl to catch the juices, use a paring knife to slice between the sections and membranes of each fruit; remove the segments whole, reserving the fruit and juice. Dice the lemon segments.

Rinse the capers well. Cover the swordfish with diced lemon and capers.

Pour half of the lemon juice on top and drizzle with a bit of extra-virgin olive oil.

Bake the swordfish at 350°F (180°C). If it gets too dry, cover it with foil.

Combine the remaining lemon juice with the oil, adding salt and pepper to taste.

Combine the mâche with the lemon-oil dressing and serve it with the swordfish.

AMBERJACK STEAK
WITH ALMOND AND PISTACHIO CRUST

Preparation time: 40 minutes   Cooking time: 10 minutes   Difficulty: easy

4 SERVINGS

1 lb. (500 g) **amberjack steaks** *(or mahi-mahi or pompano)*
1 1/2 oz. (40 g) **capers** *or about 4 1/2 tbsp.*
3 1/2 oz. (100 g) **blanched almonds** *or about 1 cup chopped*
3 1/2 oz. (100 g) **pistachios** *or about 3/4 cup whole*
4 **artichokes**
1 **bunch fresh mint**
2 **lemons**, *juiced*
1 clove **garlic**
1/3 cup plus 1 1/2 tbsp. (100 ml) **extra-virgin olive oil**
Salt and pepper *to taste*

Crush the pistachios and almonds. Remove the tough outer leaves from the artichokes. Cut them in half and remove the chokes. Slice them very thinly and put them in water with half of the lemon juice to prevent discoloration.
Cut the amberjack crosswise into thick slices. Coat the slices in the almonds and pistachios. Blend the capers with 3 1/2 tablespoons (50 ml) of olive oil. Sear the amberjack over medium heat with one-quarter of the remaining oil.
Season with salt and bake at 350°F (180°C) for 5 to 10 minutes, depending on the size of the slices. Strain the artichokes and season them with the remaining lemon juice, the remaining oil, salt, pepper and finely chopped mint.
Serve the amberjack with the artichoke salad and caper oil.

MULLET STUFFED
WITH PEPPERS, LENTILS AND PECORINO

Preparation time: 45 minutes   Cooking time: 10 minutes   Difficulty: easy

4 SERVINGS

4 **large mullet**, *cleaned and filleted (or 4 five-ounce fillets; mahi-mahi or orange roughy can be substituted)*

8 oz. (250 g) **red bell pepper**

5 oz. (150 g) **lentils**

1/3 cup (80 ml) **extra-virgin olive oil**

3 oz. (80 g) **carrots** *or about 1 1/2 small*

2 oz. (60 g) **Pecorino cheese** *(preferably Tuscan), grated*

2 1/2 oz. (70 g) **celery** *or about 2 medium stalks*

2 1/2 oz. (70 g) **onion** *or about 1 small*

1 1/4 oz. (40 g) **large black olives**, *pitted, preferably Taggiasca*

Fresh bay leaves *to taste*

Salt and pepper *to taste*

Halve bell peppers; remove stems, seeds, and membranes. Place pepper halves, cut sides down, on a foil-lined baking sheet. Bake in a 450°F (230°C) oven for 15 to 20 minutes or until skins are blistered and dark. Fold up foil on baking sheet around peppers to form a packet, sealing edges. Let stand about 20 minutes to loosen skins. With a small sharp knife, peel skin from peppers. Discard skin. Cut the peppers into slices the size of the mullet. Season them with salt and pepper. Put the lentils in cold water with the onion, carrot, celery and bay leaf. Bring to a boil and let them cook until they are very tender. Strain them and season them with salt, pepper, a dash of oil (2 teaspoons, 10 ml) and Pecorino.
Stuff the mullet with pepper slices, placing them between 2 fillets. Season with salt and pepper and arrange in a baking dish. Drizzle olive oil on top (4 teaspoons, 20 ml) and bake them for about 10 minutes. Meanwhile, blend the olives with 3 1/2 tablespoons (50 ml) of olive oil. Serve the mullet with the lentils and olive dressing.

MUSSELS MARINARA

Preparation time: 20 minutes   Cooking time: 5 minutes   Difficulty: easy

4 SERVINGS

2 lbs. 2 oz. (1 kg) **mussels**, scrubbed
7 oz. (200 g) **ripe tomatoes** or about 1 1/2 medium, peeled, seeded and diced
1/4 cup (60 ml) **extra-virgin olive oil**, plus more as needed
1/3 cup plus 1 1/2 tbsp. (100 ml) **white wine**
Fresh chopped parsley to taste
Crushed red pepper flakes to taste
1 clove **garlic**, minced
Salt to taste

Heat the oil in a pan; add the hot pepper, garlic and parsley and cook until fragrant.
Add the white wine and let it evaporate. Add the tomatoes to the pan
and after a few minutes, add the mussels and let them cook until they
open (discarding any that do not open).
Season with salt if necessary.
Serve with a drizzle of olive oil.

SCALLOPS
WITH POTATOES AND PORCINI MUSHROOMS

Preparation time: 1 hour   Cooking time: 7-8 minutes   Difficulty: medium

4 SERVINGS

4 *scallops* in the shell
1 lb. (500 g) **potatoes**
3/4 lb. (350 g) **fresh porcini
mushrooms**, thinly sliced
3 1/2 tbsp. (50 g) **unsalted butter**
1 3/4 oz. (50 g) **Parmigiano-Reggiano**,
grated (about 1/2 cup)

1 large **egg**
2 tbsp. (30 ml) **extra-virgin olive oil**
1 clove **garlic**, skin still on
1 **bunch fresh chives**
Dried breadcrumbs
Grated nutmeg
Salt and pepper

Boil the potatoes with the skins on. Drain and peel them, then mash them with a
potato ricer. Season the potatoes with salt and some grated nutmeg; add the
butter, the grated Parmigiano-Reggiano and the egg, and mix well.
Clean the scallops and save the shells (the concave part). Set the oil and the
garlic in a skillet over high heat; add the mushrooms, season with salt and
pepper, and sauté them, leaving them somewhat firm. Remove the garlic.
Get another skillet quite hot and briefly sear the scallops in it with a little oil.
Season with salt and pepper. Using a pastry bag with a medium-size rose tip,
pipe out a ribbon of potato along the edges of the shells.
Fill the prepared shells with the scallops and sautéed mushrooms.
Sprinkle with breadcrumbs, drizzle with olive oil, and cook au gratin in the oven
at 390°F (200°C) for 7 to 8 minutes. Garnish with the chives.

ROASTED SCALLOPS
WITH PURÉED PEAS

Preparation time: 35 minutes   Cooking time: 5 minutes   Difficulty: easy

4 SERVINGS

12 **scallops** *in the shell*
14 oz. (400 g) **peas** *or about 2 3/4 cups*
1/4 oz. (5 g) **cuttlefish ink** *or squid ink*
1/3 cup plus 1 tbsp. (90 ml) **extra-virgin olive oil**
Salt and pepper *to taste*

Boil the peas in salted water. Strain them and blend them in a food processor, adding a ladleful of the water they were cooked in. Then pass them through a fine-mesh sieve, which should result in a fairly dense purée. Season it with 1/3 of the oil and salt and pepper to taste. Dilute the cuttlefish ink with half of the remaining oil. Open the shells, remove the scallops and rinse them well.

Sear them in a very hot pan with the remaining oil, seasoning with salt and pepper to taste. When they're done (they should cook in about 5 minutes), serve the scallops over a layer of puréed peas. Top them with the mixture of olive oil and cuttlefish or squid ink.

SHRIMP AND SCALLOP CASSEROLE

Preparation time: 1 hour   Cooking time: 30 minutes   Difficulty: medium

4 SERVINGS

10 oz. (300 g) **scallops**
3 1/2 oz. (100 g) **shrimp**, *cleaned and shelled*
1 large **egg white**
1/4 cup (60 ml) **heavy cream**
1 **lemon**
1 tbsp. plus 1 tsp. (20 ml) **extra-virgin olive oil**
Salt and pepper *to taste*
4 **cabbage leaves**, *preferably Savoy*
1 1/2 oz. (40 g) **carrots** *or about 3/4 small, cut into thin strips*
1 1/2 oz. (40 g) **bell pepper** *or about 1/2 small, cut into thin strips*
1 1/2 oz. (40 g) **zucchini** *or about 1/2 small, cut into thin strips*

Heat the oven to 300°F (150°C).
Rinse the scallops and marinate them in a bit of oil with salt and pepper.
In a blender or food processor, whip 6 of the shrimp (leave the rest whole) with
the egg white and cream, making sure the ingredients are very cold. Season the
resulting mousse with salt and pepper.
Boil the cabbage leaves in salted water. Strain them, let them cool, dry them and
use them to line a greased loaf pan. Cook the vegetables in a large pot of
boiling salted water until just tender. Strain them and let them cool.
Remove the scallops from their marinade and add them to the shrimp mousse
along with the vegetables and reserved whole shrimp. Pour into the pan and
fold the cabbage leaves over to cover the top. Put the casserole in a hot-water
bath and bake it for 30 minutes. Let it cool, then slice and serve.

BAKED LANGOUSTINES
WITH PISTACHIOS

Preparation time: 25 minutes   Cooking time: 8 minutes   Difficulty: easy

4 SERVINGS

12   **langoustines**
3 1/2 oz. (100 g) **shelled pistachios** *or about 3/4 cup, finely chopped*
1/3 cup plus 2 tbsp. (50 g) **breadcrumbs**
2 tbsp. (30 ml) **extra-virgin olive oil**, *plus more as needed*
Salt and pepper *to taste*

Heat the oven to 350°F (180°C)
Shell the langoustines but leave the heads and tail segments attached. Season
them with salt and pepper. In a small bowl mix the pistachios with the
breadcrumbs, then add 2 tablespoons of oil and a pinch of salt. Lightly oil a
baking pan and arrange the langoustines inside. Cover them with the pistachio
and breadcrumb mixture. Bake them for about 8 minutes.

JUMBO SHRIMP
WITH TOMATO CONFIT

Preparation time: 1 1/2 hours   Cooking time: 6 minutes   Difficulty: medium

4 SERVINGS

24 **jumbo shrimp**
1 oz. (30 g) **fresh basil** *or about 1 1/4 cup whole leaves*
3 1/2 oz. (100 g) **mixed greens**
3 tbsp. plus 2 tsp. (50 ml) **extra-virgin olive oil**
2 1/2 lbs. (1.2 kg) **ripe tomatoes** *or about 6 1/2 large*
1 clove **garlic**, *thinly sliced*
1/3 oz. (10 g) **chopped fresh thyme** *or about 1/4 cup*
Salt, pepper and sugar *to taste*

Clean and shell the jumbo shrimp. Season them with salt, pepper and
2 tablespoons (30 ml) of oil and leave them to marinate.
Prepare the tomatoes by making an X-shaped incision on the bottom of each
tomato and blanching them in boiling water for 10 to 15 seconds. Immediately
dip the tomatoes in ice water, then peel them, remove the seeds and cut into
quarters. Place them on a baking sheet lined with parchment paper. Season
them on both sides with thyme, garlic and a pinch of salt, pepper and sugar.
Bake at 175°F (80°C) for 1 hour.
Line another baking sheet with parchment paper and arrange square baking
molds on top. Fill them with alternating layers of tomatoes and shrimp. Finish
with a layer of tomatoes. Bake in the oven at 300°F (150°C) for 6 minutes. Blanch
the basil leaves in a small amount of boiling salted water for a couple of
minutes. Strain them and put directly in ice water. Use an immersion blender to
blend them with the remaining oil. Remove the molds from the oven and serve
the shrimp and tomatoes with the basil oil.

SEAFOOD SKEWERS
IN SALMORIGLIO SAUCE

Preparation time: 45 minutes   Cooking time: 10 minutes   Difficulty: easy

4 SERVINGS

8 **scallops**
8 **shrimp**, shelled and deveined
7 oz. (200 g) **monkfish fillet**
2 mullet, about (200 g) **each**, cleaned, filleted, and cubed (orange roughy or sea bass can be substituted)
2 **lemons**, juiced
1 clove **garlic**, minced
1 tbsp. (4 g) **minced fresh parsley**
1 tsp. (4 g) **fresh oregano**
3/4 cup plus 1 1/2 tbsp. (200 ml) **extra-virgin olive oil**
3 1/2 tbsp. (50 ml) **hot water**
Salt and pepper to taste

Slide the cubes of monkfish onto 8 skewers, alternating with the scallops, shrimp and mullet. Start the salmoriglio by pouring the oil into a bowl. Add the lemon juice and hot water, whisking vigorously. Add the garlic and parsley. Heat it in a bowl of a double boiler (or in a heatproof bowl set over [not in] a pan of simmering water) for 5 to 6 minutes, whisking continuously.
Drizzle some salmoriglio sauce over the skewers. Grill them, basting with more salmoriglio as they cook. Season them with salt and pepper.
Top them with the remaining salmoriglio and serve.

ADRIATIC FISHERMAN'S BROTH

Preparation time: 40 minutes   Cooking time: 30 minutes   Difficulty: medium

4 SERVINGS

11 oz. (300 g) **monkfish**, *cut into chunks*

4 medium-size **red mullet**, *about 14 oz. (400 g) each*

4 **prawns** *(or large shrimp)*

7 oz. (200 g) **scorpion fish**, *cut into pieces (substitute striped bass or red snapper)*

20 **clams**, *scrubbed*

20 **mussels**, *scrubbed and debearded*

3 1/2 oz. (100 g) **squid**, *cleaned and sliced into rings*

7 oz. (200 g) **onion**, *chopped*

3 1/2 oz. (100 g) **celery**, *chopped*

2 cloves **garlic**, *chopped*

1 tbsp. (4 g) **chopped fresh parsley**

2 tbsp. plus 2 tsp. (40 ml) **extra-virgin olive oil**

16 **slices rustic bread**, *toasted*

Salt and pepper *to taste*

In a large skillet, sauté the mussels and the clams in a little bit of water with the lid on. As soon as they open, set them aside, then filter the cooking liquid through a fine-mesh sieve and set that aside.

Heat the olive oil in a large skillet and sauté the onion, garlic and celery. Add the squid and, after a few minutes, add the whole red mullet and the scorpion fish. After 5 minutes, add the monkfish. Pour in the cooking liquid from the mussels and clams, add salt and pepper to taste and finish the cooking, which should take about 30 minutes in all. Lastly, add the mussels and clams.

When cooked, sprinkle broth with the parsley. Serve with the slices of rustic bread.

MIXED FRIED FISH

Preparation time: 30 minutes   Cooking time: 5 minutes   Difficulty: medium

4 SERVINGS

1 lb. (450 g) **squid**
8 3/4 oz. (250 g) **red mullet**, *filleted*
7 oz. (200 g) **prawns** *(or large shrimp), shelled*
3 1/2 oz. (100 g) **fresh anchovies**, *cleaned and gutted, or canned anchovies, rinsed and dried*
5 1/3 oz. (150 g) **sardines**, *cleaned and gutted, or canned sardines, rinsed and dried*
2/3 cup (100 g) **semolina flour** *or all-purpose flour*
Vegetable oil for frying, *as needed*
Salt *to taste*

Prepare the squid; wash and separate the tentacles. Cut the body of the squid into rings (if the squid is small it can even be left whole).
Heat the oil in a large skillet until hot and shimmering.
Dip the various types of fish in the flour and fry them separately, making sure that the oil does not overheat. Remove the fish from the oil with a skimmer and let drain on parchment paper. Season with a pinch of salt and serve.

SEA BREAM FILLET
IN BELL PEPPER AND SEAFOOD SAUCE

Preparation time: 40 minutes   Cooking time: 10 minutes   Difficulty: medium

4 SERVINGS

2 lbs. 3 oz. (1 kg) **sea bream** *(or striped bass)*
1 lb. (500 g) **yellow bell pepper** *or about 2 1/2 large, thinly sliced*
8 oz. (250 g) **yellow onions** *or about 2 1/2 medium, thinly sliced*
1 **sprig fresh thyme**, *stripped*
1 lb. (500 g) **mussels**, *cleaned and debearded*
12 **cooked shrimp**
1 tsp. (4 g) **minced parsley**
Salt and white pepper *to taste*
1 1/2 tsp. (8 ml) **extra-virgin olive oil**

Drizzle 1 teaspoon (5 ml) of oil in a pan over low heat and sauté the vegetables and thyme. Add a few tablespoons of water and cook until vegetables are tender. Purée them and pass the purée through a fine-mesh strainer. Clean and scale the fish. Slice it into fillets and cut each one into 4-inch (10 cm) diamond shapes. Put the mussels in a pot with just a bit of water over high heat and cover with a lid. When mussels have opened, strain them and remove the shells. Filter the remaining liquid from the pot and set it aside. Sear the sea bream in a nonstick pan with a bit of oil, starting with the skin side down. Season it with salt and pepper, then turn it over and cook it on the other side for a couple of minutes. Remove the fish and deglaze the pan with the liquid from the mussels. Strain the resulting sauce and mix it with the pepper-and-onion purée. Serve the sea bream in the sauce, with shrimp and mussels on the side. Top everything with parsley and ground white pepper.

STUFFED CALAMARI

Preparation time: 30 minutes   Cooking time: 15 minutes   Difficulty: medium

4 SERVINGS

4 **medium squid**
4 **shrimp**, peeled and deveined
1/3 cup (40 g) **breadcrumbs**
Zest and juice from 1 **lemon**
1 large **egg white**
1/2 clove **garlic**, minced
1 tbsp. (4 g) **minced fresh parsley**
3 1/2 oz. (100 g) **mixed greens**
3 tbsp. (40 ml) **extra-virgin olive oil**
Salt and pepper to taste

Cut the tentacles off the squid and boil them in water with the lemon juice.
Roughly chop the tentacles and finely chop the shrimp.
Mince the garlic and parsley. Combine the garlic, parsley, breadcrumbs, egg white, tentacles, shrimp, a pinch of lemon zest and salt and pepper to taste.
Stuff the squid with this filling, using toothpicks to hold them closed.
Lightly oil a baking pan and arrange the squid inside. Bake them in the oven at 350°F (180°C) for about 15 minutes.
Place mixed greens on 4 plates. Slice the squid and place each serving atop the greens. Top it off with a drizzle of olive oil.

BRAISED CUTTLEFISH

Preparation time: 30 minutes   Cooking time: 45 minutes   Difficulty: easy

4 SERVINGS

1 3/4 lbs. (800 g) **cuttlefish** (or squid)
3 1/2 tbsp. (50 ml) **extra-virgin olive oil**
1 **bunch fresh parsley**
5 1/3 oz. (150 g) **onions** or about 2 small, chopped
2 1/2 oz. (70 g) **celery** or about 2 medium stalks, chopped
1 clove **garlic**, chopped
10 oz. (300 g) **Swiss chard**, roughly chopped
1/3 cup plus 1 1/2 tbsp. (100 ml) **dry white wine**
Salt and pepper to taste

Wash the chard but don't dry it. Put the wet chard (don't add any water) in a covered pot with a pinch of salt. Let it cook over low heat for a few minutes.
Carefully clean the cuttlefish or calamari and cut them into strips.
Heat the oil in a large skillet and sauté the onion, celery and garlic until golden brown. Add the cuttlefish. Pour in the white wine and let it evaporate. Continue to cook, adding a few drops of water if necessary. When the cuttlefish is very tender, in about 1 to 2 minutes, add the chard. Season with salt and pepper and serve.

STUFFED CUTTLEFISH

Preparation time: 40 minutes   Cooking time: 30 minutes   Difficulty: easy

4 SERVINGS

1 3/4 lb. (800 g) **cuttlefish** *(or squid)*
7 oz. (200 g) **dried breadcrumbs**
1 3/4 oz. (50 g) **grated Pecorino cheese**
2 **eggs**
1 clove **garlic**, *finely chopped*
1 tbsp. (4 g) **finely chopped fresh parsley**
1 3/4 oz. (50 g) **salted capers**, *rinsed well and finely chopped*
1/3 cup (80 ml) **extra-virgin olive oil**
2 3/4 oz. (80 g) **black olives**, *chopped*
7/8 cup (200 ml) **white wine**
Salt and pepper *to taste*

Clean the cuttlefish, without tearing them in half. Remove the bone, the ink sack
and the insides, the skin and the eyes. Wash well under running water and drain.
In the meantime, prepare the stuffing. Finely chop the cuttlefish tentacles and
mix together with the garlic, parsley, olives and the capers. Beat the eggs in a
bowl with the Pecorino cheese, salt and pepper.
Add the breadcrumbs and the previously chopped ingredients.
Mix well to obtain a smooth mixture. Stuff the cuttlefish with the mixture and
close with a toothpick. Place the cuttlefish in a lightly oiled baking dish, splash
with wine and bake at 400°F (200°C) for about 30 minutes.
Remove from the oven and cool for a few minutes before serving.

SMALL CUTTLEFISH WITH PEAS

Preparation time: 20 minutes   Cooking time: 40 minutes   Difficulty: easy

4 SERVINGS

1 3/4 lbs. (800 g) **small cuttlefish**, *cleaned and halved lengthwise (or squid)*
5 1/3 oz. (150 g) **onions** *or about 2 small, chopped*
1 clove **garlic**, *chopped*
1 **bunch fresh basil**, *thinly sliced*
1/3 cup plus 1 1/2 tbsp. (100 ml) **extra-virgin olive oil**
1 tbsp. (4 g) **minced fresh parsley**
5 1/3 oz. (150 g) **tomato purée**
1/3 cup plus 1 1/2 tbsp. (100 ml) **white wine**
Salt and pepper *to taste*
5 1/2 oz. (160 g) **peas** *or about 1 cup*

Sauté the onion with the oil in a saucepan over medium heat. Add the cuttlefish and the garlic and cook for a couple of minutes. Pour in the white wine and let it evaporate. Add the tomato purée, peas, parsley and basil. Season with a pinch of salt and pepper and cook until the cuttlefish is very tender.

OCTOPUS WITH POTATOES

Preparation time: 15 minutes   Cooking time: 2 1/2 hours
Cooling: 1 hour   Difficulty: easy

4 SERVINGS

1 lb. (500 g) **octopus**
1 lb. (500 g) **potatoes**, *peeled*
1 **onion**, *about 5 oz. (140 g)*
1 **carrot**, *about 1 1/4 oz. (35 g)*
3 **stalks of celery**, *about 2 oz. (55 g), trimmed*

3 oz. (80 g) **black olives**
1/3 cup plus 1 1/2 tbsp. (100 ml) **extra-virgin olive oil**
1 **lemon**, *juiced*
1 tbsp. (4 g) **chopped parsley**
Salt and pepper *to taste*

Bring a pot of salted water to a boil, add the onion, carrot, and one stalk of celery. Cook for 5 minutes, then place the octopus in the water, making sure to dip it three times in the hot water before leaving it to cook to make it more tender.

Cook it for an hour or until it is soft; test by piercing with a knife.

After cooking, remove from heat, cover the pot, and let cool for about an hour. Meanwhile, cook the potatoes in boiling salted water for 15 to 20 minutes, or until a wooden skewer easily penetrates them. Drain, let cool, and cut them, as desired, into wedges or cubes. Also cut the remaining celery into a medium dice. Whisk together the lemon, oil, salt, and pepper until emulsified. After the octopus has cooled, drain and cut it into pieces. Then prepare the salad by mixing the potatoes, celery, black olives, and octopus. Season with the lemon-and-oil dressing and with a sprinkling of chopped parsley.

Drizzle with the remaining olive oil and serve.

OVEN-BAKED MUSSELS, POTATOES AND RICE

Preparation time: 30 minutes   Cooking time: 35 minutes   Difficulty: easy

4 SERVINGS

8 oz. (250 g) **long-grain rice**, rinsed and drained
3 oz. (85 g) **Pecorino cheese**, grated
1 1/3 lbs. (600 g) **mussels**
12 oz. (350 g) **cherry tomatoes**
10 1/2 oz. (300 g) **potatoes**, peeled and sliced

6 oz. (180 g) **onions**, sliced
1/3 cup plus 1 1/2 tbsp. (100 ml) **extra-virgin olive oil**
2-2 1/2 cups (500-600 ml) **water**
1 clove **garlic**, minced
2 tbsp. (8 g) chopped parsley
Salt and pepper to taste

Clean the mussels thoroughly, scraping under running water, then open them using a small knife. This operation should be performed over a container to collect the liquid, which will later be used in the cooking. Discard any empty shells. Cut half the cherry tomatoes into wedges, and leave the rest whole. Drizzle a bit of olive oil into the bottom of a large baking dish. Inside, arrange a layer of onions, scatter with half the garlic, parsley and cherry tomatoes. Season with salt and pepper, sprinkle the grated Pecorino over the top, and finish with half the sliced potatoes. Cover with all the rice, then arrange the mussels over the top. Make another layer with the rest of the garlic and parsley, cherry tomatoes, and cover with the remaining potatoes. Season again with salt and pepper. Sprinkle with the remaining grated Pecorino and drizzle with plenty of olive oil. Pour in the liquid reserved from the mussels, adding water to completely cover the ingredients. Bake the casserole (referred to in Italian as a *tiella*) at 350°F (180°C) for about 45 minutes, or until the rice is cooked to perfection.

INGREDIENTS INDEX

PHOTO CREDITS

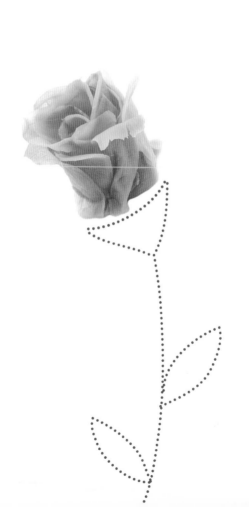

The Taunton Press
Inspiration for hands-on living®

The Taunton Press, Inc.
63 South Main Street
PO Box 5506, Newtown, CT 06470-5506
e-mail: tp@taunton.com

Translations:
Catherine Howard - Mary Doyle - John Venerella - Free z'be, Paris
Salvatore Ciolfi - Rosetta Translations SARL - Rosetta Translations SARL

LIBRARY OF CONGRESS CATALOGING-IN-PUBLICATION DATA IN PROGRESS
ISBN: 978-1-62710-049-6

Printed in China
10 9 8 7 6 5 4 3 2 1